SMART THERAPY™
ASSERTION

Dr Sallee McLaren, clinical psychologist and director of the Smart Therapy centre in Melbourne, Australia, has over two decades of experience helping thousands of anxious and distressed people recover without medication. With a background in brain research she has brought her extensive neurological knowledge into her daily clinical practice and has developed her own unique ST model and method of treatment. She is the author of *Don't Panic: You Can Overcome Anxiety Without Drugs*, and has recently developed an app called 'Smart Therapy' for use with mobile platforms.

SMART THERAPY™
ASSERTION

DR SALLEE MCLAREN

MUTATA
PRESS.

© Sallee McLaren 2017

First published 2017 by Mutata Press
and distributed by

Australian Scholarly Publishing Pty Ltd
7 Lt Lothian St Nth, North Melbourne, Vic 3051

Tel: 03 9329 6963 / Fax: 03 9329 5452
enquiry@scholarly.info / www.scholarly.info

ISBN 978-1-925588-37-8

Cover design Wayne Saunders

CONTENTS

Part One:
Why Bother Learning Assertion

Part Two:
How to Become Assertive

PART ONE

WHY BOTHER LEARNING ASSERTION

FINDING YOUR
VOICE FOR LIFE

People often hear me say that learning how to be assertive is just about as important as learning how to walk. Yet there are only a small proportion of people in society who communicate assertively and even fewer who truly understand (analytically) the nuts and bolts of assertive communication. This places unassertive people at a huge disadvantage in life.

Early on in my work I saw the disastrous consequences on human interaction, career progression and intimate relationships, of not having a grasp of assertion, so I spent time observing and examining what was happening and worked-out solutions to help people, which I have now incorporated into my Smart Therapy (ST) approach. Having said that, assertion is quite complex and context-dependent so it is difficult to teach without being face-to-face and without regular over sight where subtle errors can be honed in-upon and tweaked, but obviously I will do my best here.

To begin with, over the years I have noticed that there is often a fundamental starting-error made with assertion. Most people if they are asked to explain how they perceive assertion will describe it as a mid-point on a scale between aggression and compliance – almost as if it is a compromise between these two extreme, black and white, fear and threat-driven strategies. To add further to the confusion, assertion skills are almost always taught from this perspective by health professionals running courses.

Yet, while assertion can sometimes involve compromise, it mostly does not, as it is actually about stepping over into a completely different paradigm, with a completely different set of underlying assumptions that result in new ways of viewing and operating in the world. According to ST, assertion cannot be reduced to a mid-point between two sets of extreme behaviours that conceptually belong in a totally separate paradigm.

According to ST this 'compromise' or 'mid-point' view of assertion many people hold is not correct

| Aggression | Assertion | Compliance |

The reason I believe the mid-point view is flawed, is that after examining hundreds of aggressive or compliant people in my work, I noticed that aggressive people easily flick or switch into compliance and compliant people easily flick into aggression, albeit, usually 'passive' aggression like sulking, blocking, hostility, snide comments or insulting jokes. These same people do not, however flick into assertion.

I noticed that this switching between aggression and compliance is often done when there is no *actual* threat present and therefore not the slightest need for either behaviour. Keep in mind that aggression or compliance strategies are *only* necessary when there is a *real and serious* threat of danger, and that is a very rare situation in most

Western countries once people become adults and are no longer at risk of parental threat.

This easy flicking between aggression and compliance suggests that *both* strategies belong within the same paradigm (or category) and that aggressive and compliant behaviours are just the flip-side of each other, opposite sides of the same coin, so to speak. I observed that aggression and compliance strategies were used to deal with different conflictual contexts, but the people who used them (unassertive people) seemed to have the same assumptions underlying their behaviour, and fear and perceived threat were driving their use of *both* strategies.

I noted that when faced with an opposition that is stronger and can inflict more damage, unassertive people tend to pull out their compliance strategy. On the other hand, when the opposition is perceived as weaker and able to be beaten, then unassertive people are likely to evoke an aggressive strategy as the risk of danger is lower. In both cases, unassertive people appear to have primed their brains to 'over-read' threat, hostility and danger creating a more excessive or didactic response than is actually necessary (in most cases).

In contrast, I noticed that people who used assertion as their communication strategy tended to come from backgrounds of much greater safety, where fear and threat during conflict had not been an issue. Assertive people have presumably not learnt to *over-read* threat, so they are *less reactive* to it and less likely to unnecessarily escalate, simply because they have been lucky enough not to have had to learn these responses as children. I observed that this allowed assertive people to have the luxury of being *outcome-driven* (instead of fear and threat-driven) which enabled them to more calmly seek and generally achieve win-win solutions to conflict situations.

This all fits exactly with the ST approach. People who use either aggression or compliance strategies have generally come from more threatening backgrounds where, as children, conflict was perceived as more frightening. They were unable to escape their threatening environments so they had to learn how to respond.

HOW DO WE LEARN
THE COMPLIANCE AND
AGGRESSION STRATEGIES?

If we encounter high levels of frightening threat and conflict before we get to our early to mid-twenties (when we reach full-brain development) then we respond in a similar way to how other animals with smaller frontal brains behave when they encounter serious threat. They either fight ferociously and aggressively for survival or to their death, or alternatively they 'freeze' and play dead or hide, trying not to be noticed by the predator.

When children have to live within threatening environments they nearly always, very sensibly adopt the compliance option, because it keeps them alive and often allows them to hide undetected by the threat. Frequently, the threat comes from someone bigger than them, and is often an aggressive parent who has an unpredictable and short fuse, but with whom they are forced to cohabitate. In my clinical experience, this is how the compliance strategy is learned.

The aggression strategy appears to be learned usually during adolescence when two important things change. Firstly, children get much bigger and may now be taller and more physically powerful than their parents. Secondly, much more frontal brain comes online and teenagers attach more strongly to their peer group, providing them with more independent thinking and less reliance for perspective, upon their parents. With more frontal brain teenagers get more logical and rational, allowing for more emotional distance from their parents, making them able to appraise their parents (and other things) more objectively.

In learning the aggressive strategy, what usually happens (and I have heard hundreds of slightly different versions of this *one* story) is that there is an aggressive and unpredictable parent who is still in the teenager's face screaming at them and bullying them, even by the time they reach adolescence.

When teenagers are pushed to respond to these high levels of aggression, then instead of going compliant as per usual, the adolescents 'under threat' are forced to think slightly out of the square and realise that they are actually as big as their parents. Then having more cognitive independence, they will suddenly, in the moment of threat, dig deep in courage (or feel they have nothing to lose) and fire back with even more malice than the aggressive parents. At this point, the aggressive parents suddenly realise that they have out-of-control teenagers, who might be stronger than them, on their hands, and the aggressive parents quickly switch into compliance mode and back away physically or back down verbally.

Suddenly, the teenagers think 'A ha – that's what I have to do to survive threat: I have to get *even more* frightening and *even more* ferocious than the enemy and then the enemy will cower to me'. At that moment, the teenagers have learnt the aggression strategy and they will start to use it often and in many contexts, enjoying the greater sense of power that it delivers compared with the compliance strategy.

But not all compliant children become aggressive adults. For various reasons, some adolescents never learn the aggression strategy. This may occur when there are payoffs for children in remaining compliant, such as observing the frightening, intense and often violent interactions occurring between aggressive parents and other siblings (because bullying parents don't *always* back down) or where alliances are able to be set-up between the aggressive parents and compliant children or teenagers. Sometimes aggressive parents will target particular children with overt abuse but form demanding (but not overtly violent) alliances with other children.

While both aggression and compliance strategies are highly problematic in life, children seem to generally (but not always) become better equipped adults if they have learned an additional set of skills through learning the aggression strategy at some stage. Aggressive adults are usually better at going out into the world and knowing and getting what they want.

On the other hand, compliant adults find navigating the world independently, very difficult, unless they form alliances with aggressive partners who can negotiate (albeit often poorly) with the wider world on their behalf. However, compliant people, lacking independent negotiating skills, are placed at a severe disadvantage during communication within these 'alliances' and are more at risk of becoming victims of domestic violence.

DEVELOPING A 'DOMINANT' PROFILE OF EITHER AGGRESSION OR COMPLIANCE

Since humans are highly brain-efficient once we learn an effective strategy (especially in our younger, formative years) we keep practising it, and if we practise it enough it will become one of our 'dominant' strategies in life, where it is so often applied that it becomes immediately 'readable' to other people and a clear part of our 'personality' profile.

At this point others might describe us as 'angry' or 'laid back', depending upon which dominant strategy we have adopted. Most of the time we keep using our strategies even when they are getting us extremely poor outcomes simply because once we learn them as 'effective' (rightly or wrongly) we tend to stop questioning their effectiveness and just keep applying them. According to ST, our 'personality' or our 'profile' is just an accumulation of our most practised learnt strategies. This makes us, as people, somewhat hit and miss and highly dependent upon our earlier, fairly random life experiences. Of course, the good news is that we can always alter, sculpt and learn new strategies at any point should we decide to change any of our more debilitating aspects.

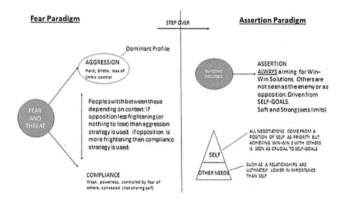

The two separate paradigms and what 'drives' them

HOW CAN PARENTING STYLES INFLUENCE OUTCOMES?

There are some exceptions to the learning processes of compliance or aggressive strategies described above. For example, in the past psychologists rarely ever saw young children who were aggressive (unless they were brain-damaged). When we did (rarely) encounter aggressive children who were not brain-damaged we knew that it was highly likely that they had been raised within very dangerous and seriously threatening circumstances.

This is because, unlike taller and more powerful adolescents, it is incredibly *risky* for younger children to develop an aggressive strategy when (threatening) adults are so much bigger and, can easily harm or kill them. Back then, it was usually only when children were pushed to within an inch of their lives and where they felt they had 'nothing left to lose' and their only chance of survival was to adopt the highly-risky aggression strategy that they did so.

Nowadays, however, parenting strategies have become alarmingly libertarian to the serious detriment of both children and their parents. Many parents are so riddled with guilt and hysterical about causing any risk of 'psychological damage' to their children that they have flicked from an **authoritarian** (aggressive) parenting style of rigid and non-contextual limits, orders, harshness, and no explanation for decisions ('my way or the highway') into a **libertarian** (compliant) style of parenting.

Libertarian parenting generally involves setting few or no limits, giving excessive and ridiculous praise to children for barely lifting a finger, waiting on children like servants, constantly orbiting children telling them till the cows come home how much they are 'loved', chasing and seeking reassurance and approval from children (who quickly learn to withhold it), and generally adopting a completely subservient and compliant demeanour towards children.

Over time this parental compliance trains children into becoming increasingly passive aggressive (sulky, arrogant, ill-mannered and contemptuous) and eventually into losing all respect for their doormat parents and becoming verbally and physically *overtly* aggressive, since there are no negative consequences placed on them for doing so. Unbelievably, in my clinic I see children as young as nine years old pushing their parents over, banging their parents' heads on the floor, kicking them, biting, scratching and screaming at them. These children will frequently tell their parents that they will contact authorities and claim they are being 'abused' if the parents attempt to take action against them.

Now I have to say that this is a completely ludicrous situation that future generations will look back upon as unfathomable! This is because the solution is actually fairly straightforward and lies in adopting *neither* an authoritarian (aggressive) nor a libertarian (compliant) approach to child-rearing. Instead, what is required is the adoption of an *authoritative* (assertive) parenting style which involves setting clear, authoritative limits with consistent negative consequences for non-adherence, but where context and rational discussion can sometimes mitigate outcomes.

The authoritative (assertive) approach always holds children's interests at heart and it is soft, kind, respectful, yet very firm, strict yet explanatory, and generally favours encouragement over punishment, but is authoritative and does not seek approval or reassurance from children. This style *only* gives *real* approval to children where they have properly earned it, and approval is certainly never given willy-nilly out of guilt or from social conformity with other parents.

Authoritative parenting does not seek to over-protect children, encouraging them to explore and try new pursuits on their own, thereby allowing them to meet real consequences in the world, both negative and positive. To make children as successful as possible (so they mostly get positive consequences) they are equipped with lots of skills from very young ages, like how to come forward and shake hands with adults, introducing themselves, making eye-contact, holding a proper and polite conversation, and finishing their conversations with phrases like 'it was lovely to meet you'.

The most likely reason that libertarian parenting has become so dominant is probably because so few people properly understand assertion. As soon as society became increasingly aware of the *dangers of child abuse*, then people automatically swung into the opposite side of the same coin with their children. Parents did not do this out of any malice or ill-will, but simply because they were genuinely trying to do the best for their children. Sadly though, setting few limits, cushioning and over-protecting children from real-life limits is within the same conceptual paradigm as being aggressive to children and it can create exactly the same negative assumptions in their young brains as hanging them up in the shed and beating them regularly.

Over-protection from the outside world teaches children ineptitude and leads to incorrect assumptions like the world is dangerous, other people are hostile, and that they are powerless to do anything about it. That is why they have to be over-protected and driven to school or never be allowed to speak with strangers. Yet stranger violence is a complete statistical rarity and nearly all violence occurs at the hands of people with whom we live.

Failure to set real world consequences (no limits) teaches children complacency, arrogance (for no good reason), and eventually aggression, and reduces their motivation to improve, often making them unskilled and ineffectual when they later hit the real world.

Children are better off equipped with genuine skills not with being warned off, over-protected, over-praised, and instructed in the language of fear, incompetence and prohibition. Keep in mind that even very young children of five years or younger are more than capable of vacuuming, sweeping, cleaning floors, doing washing and ironing (on a box or milk-crate), doing shopping, cleaning cars, tidying sheds, cooking an entire family meal, and taking full responsibility for pets as well as many other important household tasks.

Being proficient at these tasks builds children's skills and confidence and makes them stand out amongst their peers, teaching them the importance of contribution and cooperation, which will get them far better outcomes in their future lives than children who are arrogant, incompetent and sulky to boot.

THE PROBLEMS WITH
THE FEAR PARADIGM

The number one problem of operating within the fear paradigm is that *both* aggression and compliance strategies are nearly always adopted *inappropriately*. For example, it is highly appropriate to behave compliantly if we are caught up in a *non-personalised* attack, say where we happen to be randomly in a bank and it is held up at gunpoint. In this situation, the perpetrator has no personal issue with us and we will generally be unharmed so long as we don't come between them and the money – so compliance is usually the best strategy for keeping us alive in these situations.

Similarly, it is sometimes appropriate to use the aggression strategy if we are in dire, life-threatening situations where we are *personally* physically targeted, say if someone tried to abduct us at knife or gunpoint and force us into the boot of a car and clearly the intent was to seriously harm or kill us. In these types of situations, although there are massive risks and certainly no guarantees, some research suggests that outcomes are generally better if we forcefully resist at the point of initial attack rather than if we cry, freeze or try to reason with the assailant. (Keep in mind that most perpetrators are opportunists who fail to properly plan and who look for 'easy' targets offering little resistance, so offering even minimal aggressive resistance will often make their job too hard for them and drive them away.)

In the most extreme situations it may be necessary for us to take massive risks like running erratically away from a gun (to become a difficult target), behaving frighteningly and unpredictably by fiercely screaming and yelling threats at the perpetrator, or biting, elbowing, kicking, punching, using weapons, breaking fingers, or whatever it takes to escape. In these dire circumstances, an aggression strategy will not always keep us alive, but we may have a better chance of survival than if we allow ourselves to compliantly be taken to a 'second location' where the perpetrator will have full control and be able to torture or kill us in privacy.

But in reality, in Western society how often do these

highly alarming events happen in our day-to-day lives? The answer is extremely rarely, *if ever*, for most people. Yet, aggression and compliance strategies are applied widely and loosely in many peoples' daily lives.

When aggression and compliance strategies are used in the wrong context they almost inevitably lead to very poor outcomes that are lose-lose. This is the biggest problem with operating inappropriately within the fear paradigm. While people can get some small distance in life using aggression and compliance strategies, they tend to ultimately get 'stuck' and find themselves unable to move forward in achieving their life goals.

This is probably because progressing in life ultimately requires the cooperation and goodwill of other people (especially for complex problem-solving) and the assumptions that underlie the fear paradigm block most opportunities to build genuine cooperation and goodwill.

THE PROBLEMS WITH COMPLIANCE AND WHY IT RESULTS IN LOSE-LOSE OUTCOMES?

When we are compliant we generally do not ask for what we want, since we hold the underlying assumption developed in childhood that *we cannot influence outcomes by open, calm and fair negotiation*. If we had tried as children to openly discuss our needs we would have been slapped down, so being smart we go underground to prevent aggravation. We learn to hide and conceal our agenda, never openly asking for what we want and we instead try to manoeuvre events to achieve our ends.

The trouble is that if we do not openly state our objectives then we often fail to achieve them because other people simply don't notice our needs or they vaguely notice them but don't care to respond to them. This means that if we use compliance as a strategy we often miss out, we lose.

When we continually lose in life we tend to become resentful and bitter and if we feel unable to express our sense of unfairness we will harbour that resentment and it will 'leak' out in various ways severely damaging our future interactions with others. So, although we may appear relaxed and laid-back, infinitely pliable, accommodating and pleasing to others on the surface, we often become deeply stubborn, manipulative, bitter and resentful underneath.

Bitterness and resentment are easily 'readable' by others and discourage friendly cooperation. Similarly with manipulation, others dislike being treated as though they are too stupid to know what is happening and they also resist cooperation. Stubbornness results in blocking and frustrating negotiations at the nitty-gritty-putting-into-action level, because we might be saying 'yes' but digging-in and resisting any actual behaviour change, thereby impeding cooperation and often resulting in stalemate (lose-lose) outcomes.

COMPLIANCE OFTEN RESULTS IN POOR SELF-IDENTITY

Talking (the hard stuff), negotiating and arguing are some of the most important life skills that improve our mental abilities. We gradually learn to refine and articulate our views, needs and preferences by stating them out aloud to other people and then receiving crucial feedback about their strengths and weaknesses.

When compliant people fail to come forward and openly discuss these matters they fail to develop this precision and fail to define themselves clearly as people. As a result compliant people often have no definitive self-identity (sense of self) and little clue as to their likes, dislikes, ethical preferences, interests, opinions or what they stand for in life. This makes them more likely to 'follow' others to fit-in and conform irrespective of the agenda. With only weak internal direction, compliant people can often be manoeuvred by more powerful others who have clearer, more defined objectives.

This means that aggressive people interacting with compliant people often get their way over many matters, especially more trivial ones. However, aggressive people will still get blocked and stubbornly resisted on larger, longer-term goals that require significant behaviour change from compliant people. This frustrates and confuses aggressive people who cannot understand why behaviour change is not forthcoming when verbal agreement has apparently been reached. Compliant people can be very effective at passively blocking, digging-in, resisting and spoiling results and ending up with lose-lose outcomes.

THE LIES OR SELF-DECEIT OF COMPLIANCE

In my work, I have noticed that nearly always when compliant people are asked why they refuse to openly discuss differences and why they appear to cave-in to others' demands they claim it is because they 'care' about other people and prefer to let them have their way. They often describe themselves as soft, helpful, generous and kind to others.

However, when we put this apparent 'caving-in-but-actually-deeply-stubborn-with-refusal-to-talk-openly-behaviour' under the microscope, we see that it is exactly the opposite of these favourable attributes. If we really feel kind, soft, generous, and cooperative, and if we truly hold another person's interests *genuinely* at heart then we want them to do as well as they possibly can in life.

The more we love people and the closer we are to them, the more we want the best for them. In order for people to do well in life they have to be able to continually learn and progress because if they get 'stuck' they fall by the wayside unable to progress and they usually become demoralised, depressed, anxious, addicted, angry or resentful.

When we comply and fail to come forward and openly discuss differences of opinion and fail to set proper limits we actually deprive other people of important opportunities to learn and move forward. Others simply keep repeating their seriously problematic behaviours because there are no consequences being put in place by compliant people.

The reason people depend upon external limits to learn is because we are *all* born into imperfect environments and therefore we *all* build imperfect brains that are limited by our individual 'imperfect' experience. This means we have blind-spots, often huge ones! In a sense we are all trapped in our own prison cell and we require cooperation and assistance from others to help us find the way out. In many situations in life, we need a brain outside our own brain.

It is very common not to know when we are making

mistakes until the limitations of our mistakes are pointed out to us. Often it is only the people who truly love and care for us who are willing to sufficiently 'invest' in us who bother to explain our limitations to us. We all need to be aware that the biggest lies are always those that we tell ourselves in the privacy of our own heads simply because we only know what we know with one (limited) brain.

External limits are the main tool we have at our disposal that can mitigate much of our imperfect brain problem, providing us with all-important feedback. If we are prepared to absorb that feedback then we can genuinely gain insight and progress in life.

In other words, we *all* require external limits. By setting no limits and failing to openly talk about differences and problematic behaviour we fail to genuinely care for other people. If we truly feel soft, kind, generous and cooperative with other people we do *not* cave-in. Caving-in has been incorrectly labelled in the minds of compliant people as 'soft' when it is actually 'weak' – a clear example of self-deceit. Assertive limit-setting is true softness. This is why authoritative and assertive parenting (mentioned earlier) is genuinely in the true interests of children.

When we fail to set proper limits in our interactions with others we are teaching them that there are no problems with their actual problematic behaviour. In effect we are saying 'keep on doing that, it is fine with me'. This is not only misguiding and deceitful but it also robs other people of the opportunity to learn to behave differently.

In these types of situations people using compliant strategies 'lose' because they have to endure ongoing and (perhaps escalating) problematic behaviour from others. However, other people interacting with them also 'lose' the opportunity to gain insight, which keeps them repeating behaviours that often give them very poor outcomes and increase their chances of getting 'stuck' in life.

COMPLIANCE, DEEP STUBBORNNESS AND USELESS TREASURE CHESTS

As I have already mentioned, stubbornness can be a huge problem when people adopt compliance as their dominant profile. Even though it is often held up like a badge of honour supposedly reflecting 'strength of character', stubbornness actually reflects a deeply, closed-mind that is *impermeable* to persuasive evidence. It reflects a mind that is 'stuck' and unable to progress. This is not something of which to be proud.

Yet, it is something that is completely understandable and rational. Compliant people frequently feel that they have given up everything else of themselves to others, placating, pleasing and accommodating, so naturally they are proud of holding-out over certain matters. However, to hold onto these parts of themselves, they have to hide them and not reveal their existence or they believe (more powerful) others will find them and confiscate or belittle their 'treasures'. These 'dirty little secrets' are kept tightly hidden, concealed in the dark, like a treasure chest which they believe contains their 'true' sense of self.

Regretfully though the treasure chest nearly always contains the immature 'facts' and aspirations of a young child or teenager (depending on when compliance become entrenched as the dominant profile). The protected and heavily-guarded treasure chest contains lessons and 'facts' that are plainly incorrect, such as 'I must not reveal what I think or I will be hit' or 'I must not take the risk of saying I love someone or they will hurt me' or 'I must never disagree or I will be punished' or 'it is good to be a silent type since empty vessels make the most sound' and so on.

As a strategy, the behaviour of talking and arguing out aloud provides us with far more clarity and opportunity to revise our tightly held 'facts' or 'secrets' than vague, intangible internal mentations. Since compliant people often hold these 'secrets' within the dark treasure chest of their own minds, they rarely if ever properly see the light of day. Their opinions remain concealed and 'unshared' with their validity and credibility unchallenged over the decades. Any attempts by others to examine or unravel them are comprehensively and stubbornly blocked, leaving compliant people 'stuck', closed down and unable to move forward and learn – trapped within their own prison.

This is very different from when we operate within the assertion paradigm. In the assertion framework, we always try to keep moving forwards by continual learning. We form opinions based upon reliable, evidence and logic and we make decisions and change our behaviours in our lives upon this basis.

Most importantly, within the assertion paradigm all opinions are held open to continual scrutiny and re-appraisal (just not all at the same time!) If we encounter evidence to the contrary that is more persuasive we happily change both our view and our behaviour and when we encounter convincing evidence that reinforces our view we regard it as a basis for assuming our view is robust (but *never* absolutely certain). In other words when we operate in the assertion paradigm we are constantly open and responsive to critique and evidence.

In contrast, when we secret-away our views and opinions they fail to gain from our greater knowledge going forward in life. Without revision, many of our childhood 'facts' within the treasure chest become obsolete, outdated, unhelpful, sabotaging, incorrect and just plain silly. Yet, many compliant people continue to protect and conceal them literally to the death, having long ago lost sight or forgotten the reasons for the stubbornness in the first place.

ARE THERE ANY POSITIVES OF BEING COMPLIANT?

There are some positive aspects of compliance. People who are compliant commonly become experts at not rocking-the-boat and being sensitive to others displeasure. They are usually highly aware of nuances and can facilitate non-controversial social interaction, making social encounters go smoothly and helping others feel relaxed and at ease. However, these encounters tend to be superficial (and often boring) since more depth leads pretty much inevitably to more difference or conflict so topics are changed whenever they begin to teeter on the edge of disagreement. Which is unfortunate as conflict is interesting and provocative and enables us to learn from fruitful argument.

Compliant people tend to also be very nurturing and when other people are experiencing difficulties in life they frequently turn to compliant people to help soothe their distress and heal them. Compliant people are also often 'good citizens' helping out when others require their help and they are often able to earn the respect of others through their dedicated good works for others and the wider community.

WHY CHANGE AWAY FROM COMPLIANCE?

Despite these positives, adoption of compliance as the dominant strategy is overall a serious *losing* strategy in life. While emotionally injured people often arrive, to get nurtured and reflected back at twice their natural size, they also frequently leave because there is nothing 'real' coming back from compliant people – there is no genuine 'sharing of self'.

If people stay, it is often because compliant people have learnt an accompanying strategy of exerting subtle moral pressure. In an attempt to instil guilt into the other party, the words are generally never said by compliant people but nonetheless always implied of 'how could you do this to me when I have literally laid down my whole life for you'. This might make others resentfully stay, but do we really want others hanging around simply because they feel too guilty to leave?

As I have said, compliance prevents people from working out who they are and what they stand for in life since they are predominantly focussed on pleasing others and bending to their will in order to side-step any potential altercations which would otherwise assist them to differentiate themselves through the normal back and forth of arguments. This means there is no internal rudder steering the vessel, making it weak and subject to hijack from stronger winds.

In life, this makes it difficult to trust compliant people as their self-identity is often poorly defined and they will usually yield to stronger and more powerful others whenever necessary to escape conflict. Under pressure, when it counts compliant people are often unreliable advocates. Yet compliant people usually need to attach themselves to more powerful people who will negotiate the world for them on their behalf. The combination of these factors often means that allegiances can be switched almost overnight from one powerful 'host' to another, with the compliant person completely cutting out all connection with previous alliances.

While compliant people can be seen as 'active' in both their attachment and stubborn resistance to more powerful others they are ultimately passive passengers in life who are continually subject to others demands. We only get one chance at life and compliance provides no self-direction or self-identity and it relies on the unreliable goodwill (or guilt) of more powerful others.

While cooperation appears to be taking place, there is no *genuine* willingness from compliant people to openly share views and opinions since to do so would risk potential conflict. This means that there is no real 'knowing' of the compliant person and nothing 'real' coming back from them, so there is nothing to stay attached to or 'in-love' with. Being in a relationship with a compliant person is not that dissimilar to being in a relationship with yourself.

Moreover, as mentioned, when compliant people do not set clear limits others cannot learn and improve, often becoming worse and worse, as there are no consequences put in place for problematic behaviours. For example, when there are no limits set, the other party can get more and more aggressive until they become 'abusive' not because they are intrinsically 'bad' people but simply because when there are no fences put up people tend to walk on the grass.

Over time, without improvement and progress, partners of compliant people become equally as stuck with these types of lose-lose outcomes. Despite the guilt often applied by compliant people, partners frequently leave them, not out of malice, but in order to save themselves from stagnating and dying alongside them.

WHY DOES AGGRESSION RESULT IN LOSE-LOSE OUTCOMES?

While compliance clearly results in dreadful outcomes, adoption of the aggressive strategy has major limitations also. Aggression immediately gets others offside, preventing cooperation because people on the receiving end hate being unnecessarily agitated, escalated, threatened or coerced. So while others may 'appear' to comply with the aggressor, they actually stubbornly and passively block and resist any long-term outcomes or deeper change. This frequently leaves the aggressive person completely confused and nonplussed since agreement 'appears' to have been reached on the surface since the compliant person has said 'yes' or nodded their head in 'apparent' agreement but then (confusingly) resists any deeper or longer-term behavioural change whatsoever.

This *lack of insight* on the part of the aggressor goes right back to adolescence when the strategy was first learned.

All those years ago when the bullying parent appeared to back down, the teenager *mistakenly* formed the assumption that the aggressive parent had complied (as evidenced by them backing down). From the 'display' of compliance the teenager then assumed that the bullying parent had genuinely changed and would now acquiesce.

But there are many ways to skin a cat, and the bullying parent was able to find many other ways of passively blocking the teenager while still maintaining high levels of (more concealed) hostility. In other words, the hostility had just been pushed underground and out-of-sight.

Although the teenager believed they had achieved a 'win' outcome, in reality, all that the teenager achieved was to stop the *immediate* danger of being screamed at or physically hit. Of course, this was an important outcome in the circumstances as it stopped the *physical* violence and this is why aggression can be the appropriate response in actual one-off, life-threatening events.

However, a 'true' win-win for both the teenager and the bullying parent would have been for the parent to *genuinely* learn (gain insight) through friendly persuasion with the teenager that it is ultimately in their own best interests to cooperate and uncover the basis or reason for any hostility. Then that hostility could have been resolved through honest and controlled talking, planning and behaviour change. Such a response would then have likely resulted in *genuinely* changed feelings and behaviours allowing the bullying parent (of their own accord) to become more kind, soft and loving towards the teenager. The teenager, feeling the hostility evaporate would then calm down immediately and reciprocate with kindness and highly cooperative behaviours, which would ultimately 'nurture' the bullying (scared) adult placing both parties into a virtuous rather than vicious cycle.

Sadly, inappropriate adoption of the aggression strategy shuts down communication prematurely and prevents the achievement of these types of win-win outcomes. Aggressive people are often very verbal in their commentary, but their words, voice tone and body language are angry, blaming and abusive and their strategy is ultimately aimed at 'silencing the opposition' (shutting others up before they shut you up). This happens because even though aggressive people *appear* very confident and forthright in their verbal abuse they are actually extremely frightened underneath and see themselves as 'victims' who will be unable to influence outcomes through normal calm dialogue without escalation and 'crushing the enemy'.

ARE THERE ANY POSITIVES OF BEING AGGRESSIVE?

Despite many shortcomings aggression can be effective in some circumstances. For example, having an aggressive profile can get people quite a long way in certain contexts like organisational hierarchies, where complex interaction can often be bypassed by the linear structure of the organisation. However, aggressive people still tend to get blocked towards the top of these organisations as they cannot elicit wide enough support and cooperation for their ventures.

The aggression strategy can also teach high levels of initiative, sensitivity to opportunity and focussed, goal-directed behaviour in going after what is desired in life. In addition, because aggression 'feels' more powerful than compliance it can be a strong driver of motivation, 'apparent' courage and elevated mood. All of which make the aggression strategy an attractive option for unassertive people. Keep in mind though, that underneath the aggression strategy people still perceive themselves as 'powerless victims' even when they are flat-out bullying other people. (Recall that it is the fear and threat of conflict that is always driving both aggression and compliance strategies.)

Aggression also often helps create a stronger *sense of self* (more individuation and autonomy) than compliance, since every time we openly argue with others we are effectively saying 'You stand for such and such, and I don't agree because I stand for something different'. Over time, this helps aggressive people become more precise in defining their personal differences and preferences which set them apart from others, defining and differentiating their sense of self more clearly. But it can also lead to increased levels of isolation, as lots of practice 'going it alone' can become the default setting.

Still, the aggression strategy can result in the building of some quite impressive, charismatic, highly motivated, entrepreneurial and imposing individuals who often stand out from the crowd. However, because aggression is fear-driven these individuals often resist arguing calmly, empathically and *at length*, and they instead escalate quickly and explosively in response to conflict trying to immediately neutralise the (imagined) 'threat'. Where people over-do this strategy it can easily result in ignorant and dogmatic outcomes that are significantly less appealing.

THE LIES AND SELF-DECEIT
OF AGGRESSION

I wish I had a dollar for every time I have heard an aggressive person describe themselves as 'honest', 'forthright', a 'truth-teller' or just 'telling it like it is' when they are in reality fear-driven into being brutal, cruel and cowardly. Aggressive people are nearly always too scared to calmly and softly stay submerged in issues while full, frank and cooperative discussions occur that would otherwise lead them towards win-win solutions. Instead their escalating fear and aggressive tactics (in 'defence' of themselves as 'victims') usually turn them inadvertently into the very bullies they so often despise. Of course, bullying shuts others down making cooperation highly unlikely.

While aggressive people maintain the lie that they are the 'victims' of these encounters they will continue to blame others and remain on the offensive, ever hyper-vigilant to extinguish any potential outside 'threat'. The problem is, that once into adulthood there is very rarely (if ever) a genuine threat. Remaining inappropriately aggressive and on the offensive, with a constantly vigilant outward gaze towards potential 'threats' stops any inward, self-reflection preventing the all-important gaining of insight. We are so busy looking outward and blaming others that we fail to notice our contribution.

WHY CHANGE AWAY FROM AGGRESSION?

As a result of viewing other people as the enemy (to be ferociously eliminated) aggressive people fail to see others as ultimately being *on the same side* but with (an often small) difference to be resolved. This oppositional view of others prevents aggressive people from building openness, trust, friendliness and alliance, forfeiting their capacity for cooperation on complex issues.

In addition, aggressive people learn over time to externalise, putting the focus of their anger and blame (usually) entirely onto others. With practice aggressive people become highly efficient at going *immediately* and reflexively onto the offensive, without first appraising or reflecting upon either the relevant logical evidence being put forward or their own contribution to the situation.

In this way, aggressive people become effectively 'blind' to at least half of the pertinent information in any conflict, placing them at a huge disadvantage in terms of influencing outcomes and, it drastically increases their chances of becoming marginalised and 'stuck' in life. This profound lack of insight only worsens over the life-span as aggressive people get more proficient at their strategies, often turning from impressive, motivated individuals in their youth into lonely, ignorant, high-maintenance, closed-down bullies thereafter.

Moreover, as life progresses, there are just too many brutal and poorly controlled conflicts that effectively banish people from the realm of the aggressor. Even those that remain within the proximity of aggressive people tend to close themselves off and increasingly conceal themselves within the compliance strategy, never sharing their *true* moment by moment experiences, keeping secrets, and ultimately viewing the aggressor as the enemy.

These problems of inability to cooperate, lack of insight and driving others away either physically or mentally are some of the most colossal failures of the aggression strategy, almost always resulting in lose-lose outcomes.

Nonetheless, I find in my work, that people who have so far in life only learnt the compliance strategy must first learn the aggression strategy more overtly before they can step-over into the assertion paradigm. This is probably because operating within the assertion paradigm ultimately requires a strong sense of self, negotiating calmly, openly and vigorously with others where we must take their needs fully into account to achieve win-win solutions without losing sight of our own needs and falling back into compliance. A strong sense of self seems to be essential in this process.

DIFFERENT CONFIGURATIONS OF INTIMATE RELATIONSHIPS RELATED TO COMMUNICATION STYLES

In my work, I notice that most people who have developed an aggressive 'dominant' profile tend to partner with people who have built a 'dominant' profile of compliance. This is probably because aggressive people nearly always know what they want and they often get their way about more trivial day-to-day decisions in relationships like which movies to see, which jobs to do, or which TV shows to watch.

While people with an aggressive profile often hold compliant people in contempt for their 'weakness' they nevertheless frequently form alliances with compliant people since compliant people offer them little resistance on the smaller things in life without any clear articulation of their own. Compliant people tend to partner with aggressive people because they often lack the skills to negotiate the wider world unassisted and require an aggressive partner to go out into the world and negotiate on their behalf. In these relationships there is exchange, but it is unreliable.

For example, aggressive people often negotiate ineffectually with the wider world as their aggression and hostility diminishes trust and cooperation, often leaving the compliant person to smooth over their trail of destruction. Equally, compliant people only acquiesce on smaller and trivial issues whereas they passively resist and block mightily on bigger issues, eventually causing massive levels of frustration to aggressive people. These unresolved lose-lose barriers result in alienated and dissatisfying relationships, yet in my work I see this type of relationship configuration in about 70% of all intimate relationships.

The next most common relationship configuration (about 20%) that I see in my work are compliant people partnering with other compliant people who may live companionably side by side in life but (ultimately) remain isolated and secretive from each other. These relationships tend to be stagnant and highly alienated with no one having the initiative to drive the relationship forward or to negotiate progressive outcomes in the world.

It is only in about 5–6% of relationships that I see in my work where there are two aggressive people partnering since they tend to blow the relationship apart in fairly quick measure. Both parties are generally screaming and leaving or threatening to leave on a daily basis making these relationships untenable in the longer term.

THE HIGHLY PROBLEMATIC
ASSUMPTIONS UNDERLYING
THE FEAR-PARADIGM

Underlying the fear paradigm and the relationships built within the fear paradigm are problematic assumptions that nearly always prevent win-win solutions. In all three of the relationship styles described above the individuals remain unnecessarily emotionally *reactive* to conflict making the parties respond in kneejerk ways (like getting furious or shutting down and hiding) instead of taking the time to calmly consider their mutual problem and their preferred outcomes or solutions. In this reactive state, arguments are often poorly communicated and then taken *personally*. Within the fear paradigm parties often perceive themselves as just trying to 'survive' instead of learning the fun and pleasure in negotiating in a relaxed, reasoned manner.

Parties also generally hold many simply inaccurate assumptions such as that their partner is the *enemy on the opposing side* blocking cooperation from the outset and resulting in alienated, frustrating and ineffectual interactions and relationships. As a result of these 'enemy' assumptions within the fear paradigm, all parties are concealing their agenda as well as *shutting down fluid communication* through either ferocious aggression (stamping on the opposition before they stamp on you), or through compliance (by being too meek and/or poorly internally directed to identify either problems or possible solutions). In both cases issues are not dealt with and are swept under the carpet, failing to be properly resolved.

In addition, all parties within the fear paradigm hold assumptions about being powerless *victims* believing (usually incorrectly) that *others are more powerful* and that they *cannot influence outcomes openly* through transparent, on-the-table genuine persuasion and argument. As a result people operating within the fear paradigm instead use either force (if aggressive) or manipulation/guilt (if compliant) to try and meet their needs. However, by continuing to hold victim assumptions and keeping on with the derived behaviour, people within the fear-paradigm fail to learn that they can nearly always influence outcomes very effectively.

Moreover, both parties in perceiving themselves as victims *fail to take proper responsibility* for their own contributions and persist in *blaming each other* at every juncture. Unfortunately, this leaves very little chance of actually solving the problem, since the 'blamer' is so busy looking outwards they never even notice their own 50% contribution to the problem – so it cannot be rectified. To make matters worse, others who are getting 'blamed' frequently get so defensive that it is almost impossible for them to properly self-reflect so their 50% also goes unrectified.

You don't have to be Einstein to realise that with 100% of the problem not addressed there is very little chance of solving it. In fact, these problematic assumptions underlying both aggression and compliance profiles generally irreparably block and damage negotiations from the outset and lead pretty much unfailingly to lose-lose outcomes.

THE HIGHLY EFFECTIVE ASSUMPTIONS UNDERLYING THE ASSERTIVE PARADIGM

In my work, the relationships I most rarely observe (perhaps about 4–5%) but which are by far the best relationships I ever see, are when both parties are assertive. Underlying the assertion paradigm and the relationships built within it are highly effective assumptions that foster cooperation and win-win solutions to even the most difficult problems. It probably will not surprise you to realise that these assumptions are entirely different (polar opposites) to those held within the fear paradigm.

In these cases both individuals see themselves as *on the same side* but just with some differences and conflicts to resolve. All parties are *proactive* and so they are *non-reactive* and therefore arguments are communicated and taken in *non-personalised ways*, keeping *communication open* and fluid. At a fundamental level both parties see their *interests as completely aligned*, and they want the other party to do as well as they possibly can and are willing to help in whatever ways they can to achieve the best outcomes for their partner. Basically, they see their interests as so much aligned that they regard a 'great' outcome for their partner as a 'great' reflection on them for helping achieve it.

In this way, the parties are *highly cooperative* in achieving their very 'best' shared visions which are initially vigorously argued out and gradually tweaked and improved over time. They operate as a *team* in life, but with completely autonomous and independent mental processes; extremely close but not 'needy'. They don't agree because they are enmeshed, joined at the hip or compliant, but rather because they have argued and ironed out any earlier conflicts and are now in *genuine* agreement about the way forward.

Since parties see themselves as fundamentally on the same side, and *never* as the opposition or the enemy, issues can be argued out vigorously and as quickly as possible to achieve fast resolution. *Kindness, fairness and egalitarian values* are central to the assertion paradigm, and it is just assumed that each party has requirements to be met and aspirations to fulfil that require fair and equal time for problem-solving and treatment.

It is also always assumed that each party can equally and *strongly influence outcomes*, so there is an optimistic approach taken to every argument where both people just take it for granted that they will get an excellent solution or, that further discussion is needed to find that excellent solution if one has not yet been reached. There is never any notion that either party will somehow get 'ripped-off' because both parties are open and clear advocates for themselves *and* each other.

In the assertion paradigm, resolution of conflict is always handled through controlled, ruthlessly rational, at times intense but nearly always enjoyable, *non*-personal argument. Differences are often dealt with playfully, kindly and with curiosity. Even personal issues are dealt with often from the perspective of what is most in the *genuine best interests* of the other party.

For example, 'You know I love you madly and you

are a truly wonderful person, but when you raise your voice I don't think it helps you get good outcomes. I noticed for example, that Jenny pulled away from you and sulked last time it happened, and that upset you afterwards and led to you feeling bad about yourself. Looking at it from outside your brain, I don't think that raising your voice is helping you move forward in life – in fact, I think it is keeping you 'stuck' as there have been many repetitions of the scenario with Jenny just getting played out over and over. I think we need to work out why you might have first learnt to raise your voice (so we can both better understand the behaviour) and also work out how you can stop doing it. Also, when it happens and you raise your voice with me, I think that I might be contributing to the problem by not objecting early enough, so I think I also need to focus on this so I can fix up my part as well. Also, because this is an old, established habit it probably feels completely normal to you, so maybe there is some way I can help alert you to your behaviour when you are not aware you are starting to escalate. Maybe when I notice that you reach 3/10 I give you a 'calming down' signal that you *ensure* you take notice of. Could that work?'

In assertive relationships, both parties clearly understand that there is no such thing as a 'win' for them as individuals if the other party 'loses', since their apparent win will be undermined, resisted and resented resulting in re-evoking the fear paradigm and lose-lose outcomes. This means that all possible solutions that are put forward are genuine win-win solutions for all parties. Then these solutions are discussed at length and a way forward is chosen and clearly agreed upon. The chosen solution is then tested-out in life for its effectiveness by both parties changing their behaviour as agreed and assessing the results. If solutions are found to be ineffective then new interventions are put in place instead and similarly discussed, tested and evaluated.

There is a complete absence of 'blaming others' or the 'powerless victim' assumption in the ST assertion paradigm. (ST assertion is a teleological not deontological paradigm and subject to the same conditions discussed at the beginning of Chapter 4 in my book *Quit Anxiety*

Now.) Each party easily takes responsibility and identifies their own (and the other party's) 50:50 contribution to any mutual problems or conflicts and each party undertakes (if persuaded) to change their behaviour in an attempt to rectify the issue. Both parties monitor the outcomes and interventions are tweaked as necessary.

Since issues are usually quickly resolved with vigour and friendliness there is minimal harboured resentment or bitterness and couples are much more likely to be very in-love, especially as the decades pass and every genuine resolution of conflict results in evermore closeness and intimacy. Love becomes deeper over time with increasing commitment and investment in each other's lives, effectively building trust, empathy and safety for both parties.

PART TWO

HOW TO BECOME ASSERTIVE

KARL POPPER AND ROBUST RATIONAL PARADIGMS

I have based the ST assertion model to some extent on the work of Karl Popper who was an Austrian philosopher of science (1902–1994) who strongly promoted *critical rationalism*. He argued that the reason why science has been unbelievably successful as a paradigm is because scientists continually subject their hypotheses (theories) to robust critique through experimentation, testing of the null hypothesis, and rational debate. In other words, scientists do their upmost to *disprove* their own ideas through robust testing and critique.

In ST assertion we similarly aim for the very best we can do rather than aiming for the lowest common denominator often achieved through inept compromise. We put up all manner of ideas and possible solutions to problems and conflicts, and then debate their merits freely and vigorously. We accept robust anomalies and evidence to the contrary and rationally try to work out how they might be accounted for or incorporated. This approach constantly moves us on as both individuals and in terms of wider social and cultural progress.

This approach frees us from being personally over-attached to stubbornly held views and enables us to keep open minds as no view is ever strictly regarded as 'proven' and may, with more robust knowledge, be found to be completely wrong at some later stage. Of course, we do our very best in deciding which view is the most robust (given tight logic and the evidence at hand) and then we put it into action to test its validity over and over again, looking for shortcomings that we then correct and incorporate. With this approach we accept that despite our best efforts, no solution will ever be perfect and we will probably never obtain the 'absolute' truth yet we will be doing the best that we can given what we currently 'know'.

This allows us to argue with free licence. We can relax and detach more from our ideas, seeing them as separate from ourselves and just one of many ideas we could potentially put forward. We are free to say the most outrageous things and then simply retract them if they are found to be too silly! Some ideas will have merit and some will not, but who cares really, because no one actually knows if ideas have merit *until* they are put under the microscope and debated. In the first instance we all have as much right as each other to put up our views and test them out. Amazingly though, the more we subject our arguments to open-slather scrutiny the more they become *genuinely* robust.

With this ST assertion approach, we stop being personally over-attached to specific outcomes allowing us to effortlessly change our minds. We argue with varying degrees of commitment depending upon the extent to which our views have already withstood rational critique and testing. We would argue with much lower levels of commitment when our ideas have not yet been subjected to robust argument, for example, 'I'm not at all sure of this, but tell me what you think of this idea'.

On the other hand, we do not cave-in *unless we are genuinely persuaded* otherwise this would just be compliance and we are back then operating within the fear paradigm. We ought to argue quite vigorously especially if our idea is highly logical and rational and it has already withstood robust critique.

Equally, it does not matter a scrap if we don't always argue at our very best. Poor delivery of argument does not automatically mean we have poor content. On occasion where we fail to perform well in debate, we can always come back to the discussion at a later date with more considered arguments. Over time, as we relax and start to really enjoy argument we get better and better at performing and critiquing in the moment of debate.

However, as soon as a more robust solution is put forth then we ought to embrace it and *happily* drop our own view, *genuinely* shifting our mind-set (not stubbornly going underground). When we are unattached to ideas and do not see them as part of our self-identity we can easily let them go and choose better alternatives that will keep us open and progressing in life. This means that even when we 'appear' to lose an argument we actually 'win' because we have moved forward in our learning and we now hold a more robust view than we did previously. We can be genuinely happy when we say 'OMG! You are just *so* right, I never thought of it that way before. Thank you!'

ASSERTION IS NOT
JUST FOR RESOLVING
CONFLICT WITH OTHERS

Once we step over into the ST assertion paradigm it becomes a way of life. It is not just for using when there are issues of conflict with others. We come to use assertion principles *within ourselves* on a minute-by-minute basis whenever we feel 'internally' conflicted. This just means that we 'rationally critique' our own internal conflicts, determine to change relevant behaviours and then hold ourselves to account, rationally evaluating outcomes.

Just like in ST generally, we would engage our frontal brain and rationally critique problematic behaviours. Let's take the example of experiencing panic attacks when getting in lifts. If we were experiencing these types of panic attacks, we would feel *conflict* as we would be torn between which solution we ought to adopt: avoiding or embracing getting in lifts.

Our limbic system might 'want' us to avoid getting in lifts (because it feels scary) but our rational, frontal brain knows that avoiding lifts will increasingly shut us down in life as our brains easily generalise from lifts to cars to movie theatres to shopping centres, so instead we undertake to *happily embrace* getting in lifts going forward and to stop paying any attention to panic mentations.

In ST assertion we regularly appraise our internal conflicts and subject them to robust rational critique to determine rational solutions. We then implement our solution and monitor its effectiveness, thereby facilitating optimal outcomes and ensuring maximum levels of self-control in life.

HOW DO WE
LEARN SMART THERAPY
ASSERTION?

Just by having a human brain with its enormous frontal capacity for rationality and comprehensive mental control we are already halfway there. On top of this we now have some clear understanding about ST assertion and the theory it is based upon. As a result, we can endeavour to keep ourselves aligned and consistent with that theory. In addition, I will now provide a vignette and then offer a few other 'tips' about how we 'live it' in day to day situations.

THE MARY AND TONY STORY

Tony and Mary have a conflict around smoking. Tony smokes and Mary does not smoke. Mary is very upset about Tony smoking as he is coughing frequently and gets bronchitis evermore often as the years pass. Tony is starting to look very unwell and his skin is looking 'grey' in colour. Mary also dislikes breathing-in cigarette smoke herself which has lately been causing her to cough more frequently.

If Mary and Tony operated within the fear paradigm they would be likely to argue explosively over the years in short bursts and then withdraw and sulk to their detriment, never properly resolving the issue. Their interaction would look something like this. Mary would beg Tony to quit and when he resisted she would become increasingly frustrated until she was agitated and angrily raising her voice.

To get Mary off his back, Tony would then pull out a compliance strategy like sulking and withdrawing but still remaining unchanged in his smoking habit. Since Mary lost control and yelled at Tony, he will now use Mary's yelling as his own personal *justification* for digging-in and stubbornly refusing to be influenced by her argument. Her yelling becomes an excuse for him to shut-down.

Alternatively, Tony might use another compliance strategy of 'appearing' to cave-in, probably also lying to himself in the process. He might swear to Mary and himself that he will quit tomorrow. Again, this will be done to get her off his back. However, the problem is that he has just caved-in and he is not yet genuinely persuaded that quitting is in *his* best interests.

This means Tony will fail to quit, he will resent it, he will tell himself he was 'forced' to do quit against his will and he will probably secretly re-start smoking within a day or two. To justify re-starting smoking when challenged by Mary, Tony is then likely to use the aggression strategy where he escalates with agitation and yells or becomes rude saying things to Mary like she is trying to 'control him' and it is 'his life' and 'if he wants to smoke he will' and she 'knows where the door is' if she 'doesn't like it'.

Mary does not want to leave so they end up with a stalemate 'compromise' where Tony ends up smoking outside in the cold so as not to affect Mary. However, this apparent 'compromise' is really a just a sad lose-lose outcome. Tony has lost because he is still smoking (and acting against his own *genuine* best interests) and Mary has lost because she is still upset and worried that Tony will die prematurely.

On the other hand, if Tony and Mary operated within the assertion paradigm the interaction and outcome would be entirely different. First of all, Mary and Tony would agree on daily times to talk at length about important matters. If they don't set aside time nothing can ever get solved. (Unassertive people frequently fail to set aside proper time for discussion and resolution because underlying their compliant and aggressive strategies is their *fear of conflict*.) Since Mary and Tony are now being assertive they might commit to going for an hour walk together every evening, or they might sit down after dinner without the TV and talk on the couch together for an hour. They may also undertake long scenic drives on weekends every so often for several hours so that they can talk *undistracted* and more deeply about major issues.

During some of their talks, Mary would most likely be the one who would raise the smoking issue with Tony because she is the 'brain outside his brain' and she can help to strengthen his frontal brain against the self-sabotaging habits of his limbic system. On other issues he will be the 'brain outside her brain'. This is because, while we all have flawed brains and habits, we do not usually have the same flawed brains and habits, so we can offer enormous assistance to one another in solving each of our limitations.

In ST assertion, there are different ways Mary might raise the issue of smoking with Tony. The first way is for Mary to *identify their problem*. For example, she might say 'We have a problem … we both love each other and want to be together and yet it breaks my heart to see you slipping away from me every day as your health diminishes with smoking'. The second way is for Mary to *own her own contribution upfront*. For example, she might say 'I am so sorry that I have not helped you with smoking earlier, I regret that and I know it has been terribly difficult for you to quit on your own, but I want to do my very best for you now because I really want us to be able to stay healthy and grow old together'.

The third way is for Mary to make a *connecting statement*. For example, she might say 'I hope you know that I love you madly, you're my very best friend of all time, but we need to tackle this smoking issue because it is causing you such terrible harm and I want you to be able to love and care for yourself as much as I love and care for you'.

The fourth way is for Mary to simply *describe the (problem) behaviour and its consequences*. For example, she might say 'When you smoke I've noticed that it stops you feeling things, making you harder and less vulnerable. Then when that happens it becomes more difficult for me to connect with you and to feel close to you. You are off alone with your cigarette. The worst thing about that is that I am your very best friend and I want to help you, in fact, more than anyone else in the world I am committed to helping you with this habit. Please understand that it is *not* a good outcome for you to push me away because I am actually your greatest ally'.

The fifth way is for Mary to show *curiosity*. For example, she might say 'How does it feel for you to have to keep satisfying urges for nicotine? Do you feel like a prisoner, held hostage to this nicotine habit? Do you think you could be happier if you could find a way to step off this unrelenting conveyor belt where you have to constantly top-up your nicotine levels to satisfy cravings? Are there ways I could help you with this?

In these conversations, Mary would be very soft and kind with Tony. It is unlikely that he would stop smoking after the first conversation and probably it would take many conversations since he has been smoking for a long time and it is a well-established habit. During these discussions Mary would ask him about why he might have started smoking in the first place. Maybe his parents divorced and no-one was taking care of him and feeling all alone he was probably an easy target for cigarette companies. Mary would be kind and understanding about how he 'feels' like he 'needs' to smoke and even that he 'loves' to smoke because that is how addictions work. She will be soft with him when he tells her that he can only imagine how 'bleak' life would feel if he did not smoke. She would be caring and understanding of how he feels like he is a 'victim' of cigarette companies, powerless and unable to quit. At the same time, Mary would gently challenge these ideas and help to free Tony from their hold.

During these talks, although Mary has the undeniable 'right' to ask Tony to go outside into the cold to smoke, within the assertion paradigm she may choose (depending on the severity of her own cough) to forfeit that right at least initially. Keep in mind that assertion is not a black and white, rule-governed paradigm it has flexibility according to context. For example, Mary would (hopefully) be emphatic and understanding about how Tony 'feels' as though he is a passive victim, unable to quit, especially as he appears to 'love' cigarettes more than life itself.

Mary has a bigger, longer-term agenda, perhaps bigger fish to fry. So rather than forcing Tony outside and risking alienation between them, she might decide it is more important to 'flag' her care for him, to demonstrate that he can stay close to her and safe, despite his difficulty with smoking. This is different from compliance, because it would not be a capitulation but rather a reasoned strategy. Unlike compliance there would be zero harboured resentment. Agreeing to Tony smoking inside would serve as a temporary indicator of goodwill, over the duration while Tony is choosing to be actively engaged in the debating process. If Tony later acted against his own best interests and disengaged from the conversation about smoking then he would receive the negative consequence of being asked to go outside to smoke.

While Mary is soft and understanding about Tony's feelings she also has a highly rational understanding of how much his feelings are undermining him and preventing him from acting in accordance his own genuine interests. As a result, she raises evidence from studies about things like how the *urges for more nicotine* simply masquerade as 'feelings' of 'love for cigarettes' and 'bleakness without cigarettes' and they will disappear at roughly the same rate as the nicotine withdrawal urges dissipate. By far the worst of the nicotine withdrawal is over in three days.

Mary will talk about how once Tony stops paying attention to cigarettes his whole brain will change and he will be able to be much happier than he has ever been in his life (especially since Tony himself spends so much time worrying about lung or throat cancer). Mary will argue that once Tony has come through the withdrawal phase (which she knows he can do by simply stopping paying attention!) he will look back and *not be able to believe* he was ever capable of harming himself so comprehensively by smoking. He will literally be a different person.

Mary might also talk softly about more difficult things like how it is one thing to (perhaps) look slightly cool smoking in your twenties, but by thirty or forty or fifty it is just starting to look inadequate. Mary will emphasise how it is not in Tony's best interests to project himself as inadequate as this will prejudice other people and then interfere with communication when they act out of pity, annoyance, condescension or contempt. Mary will argue that he is a wonderful person and ought not be treated in these ways by others but that he will need to step-up at some stage and address his 50% contribution if he wants a better outcome. She will always encourage him that he is more than capable of quitting and that she will help him at every juncture.

Mary will always exercise total mental control and she will never become aggressive, since she knows she would defeat her own argument by letting him off the hook and allowing him to dig-in with resistance, as he could then justify that she was trying to 'control him' or 'bully' him. Bit by bit, Mary will continue to go on-side with Tony, helping to strengthen his frontal brain with some of her best arguments – but always with *his* best interests at heart.

Without escalation into anger, Tony would find it difficult to resist Mary's compassionate arguments. He would come to gradually understand his smoking as an act of violence against himself and that Mary is on his side trying to help take care of him. So long as Tony was operating in the assertion paradigm he would always undertake to come forward and talk (not withdraw and sulk) no matter how difficult the topic. He would do this because he understands that he is never a victim and he cannot ever be *forced* to quit against his will. However, in the end the more rational argument about what is most in *his* genuine interests will (hopefully) prevail and Tony will win by *choosing* to quit for himself. Mary will also win because her own cough will improve and within only about five years of quitting Tony's body will have repaired itself sufficiently so that he will be healthier and he will have excellent chances of never developing lung or throat cancer or other illnesses related to smoking.

I want to now provide ten tips about how to operate in the assertion paradigm in day-to-day life. I will continue to use the Mary and Tony vignette where relevant like a template as we progress through the tips in order to explain ST assertion more fully.

TIP ONE: VOICE TONE AND BODY LANGUAGE

I would say that voice tone in particular, as well as non-verbal facial expressions and body-language (hand gestures and body posture) are crucially important (they may account for up to 85%) in achieving good win-win outcomes.

In order to have even a chance of achieving a win-win solution to the conflict about smoking Tony and Mary would have to have a strong understanding of the importance of friendly and kind voice tone and open body language. This is because these non-verbal expressions 'flag' our willingness to be open, accept responsibility, and our genuine preparedness to seek solutions to mutual problems or conflicts. Equally they can flag shut-down, closure, passive blocking, sulking, an unwillingness to accept responsibility, blaming, and no desire to seek mutual solutions. The disastrous impact of these barriers make it important to get it right!

In order to operate within the assertion paradigm, voice tone must be soft, yet strong, authoritative, friendly, relaxed and projected. If you are projecting correctly, you should be able to speak in a large hall with no microphone and no-one should ever have to ask you to repeat yourself due to lack of projection, volume or resonance. When we speak quietly we are often hiding, not owning or taking responsibility for what we are saying or alternatively we may be using a strategy of 'withholding' where we try to make others 'chase' us by having to constantly move towards us and ask for repetition.

Although in assertion we speak with plenty of projection we do not want any sharp edge in our voice. A sharp edge occurs as a result of throat constriction (tension) when our emotions become caught up in what we are saying, signalling that our limbic system is now involved. It can lead to a higher-pitched whingeing, unfriendly, angry or victim-like sound that is unpleasant for the recipient and often feels like an assault even when it is not directed personally. Interestingly the perpetrator nearly always has no clue they are doing it, yet it is *easily* readable by others and nothing drives others away faster or makes situations more likely to escalate or deteriorate.

So it is important to reflect regularly *in the moment* and ensure that we maintain voice friendliness, projection and lack of tension throughout. In ST, we always exercise frontal brain control and stay below 3/10 no matter what is happening around us. Equally, in ST assertion it is all about frontal brain control and the better we are at assertion the more we exercise incredibly strict mental discipline and *always* stay in control ensuring that any sharp edge stays *completely* out of our voice tone yet at the same time our voice is open and projected.

Although there are times in difficult or complex conflicts where our voice tone may be more intense and singularly focused, it still always remains friendly and our facial expressions are relaxed, open and spontaneous where we can easily smile and laugh with amusement at any stage.

The level of authoritativeness in voice tone is always fairly constant and indicates a willingness to take our own views seriously and back ourselves, yet it is never authoritarian, closed or dogmatic. Being authoritative in our voice means being an adult and taking proper responsibility for our views. Sometimes people can be tempted to speak in weak, childlike ways that often reflect a lack of power from childhood where a 'cute' voice may have helped to manouver safer outcomes. However, as an adult it is much more powerful and compelling to 'own' our authority in a calm and relaxed way.

Just as we would behave in relaxed, non-threatening situations, when resolving conflict we similarly keep hand gestures fluid and open, maintain relaxed eye-contact and a forward and engaged body posture as though we are interested in coming forward to solve the problem. We do not defensively 'guard' the body by rigidly folding arms (this is not a war, we are not on the defensive, this is two people with a mutual problem to solve, always to the benefit of both).

Unless it is an ultra-relaxed, informal context, we ensure we do not overly sit or lean back as this otherwise indicates withdrawal, aloofness, a desire to flee, or disengagement. Similarly we do not become mask-like and shut-down in the face or tight around the mouth or jaw as though we are 'shutting' or 'clamping' down and unwilling to share information, guarding it off from access by others.

Always central to ST assertion is the notion that as adults other people are *not* the enemy or opposition, we are on the same side we just have a problem or conflict to resolve and we are both going to find ways to win equally good outcomes – so there is nothing to actually be afraid of.

At first after operating in the fear paradigm it is difficult to achieve this crucially important voice tone and relaxed, open body language as there is initially a strong fear of interaction around issues of conflict. But fake it till you make it. Behave exactly as though you have not an iota of fear, so that anyone observing you would assume you are totally relaxed and at ease in the situation. Be like a method actor who submerges fully into role and 'becomes' the character. With a bit of practice over time you will retrain your brain so that debating out issues and finding good solutions becomes highly stimulating, amusing and great fun! Testing out and developing our ideas is one of the most enjoyable things in life!

TIP TWO: WORK OUT YOUR 'PREFERRED' OUTCOME

In my work I so often see unassertive people acting directly *against* their own best interests. This is often because when we operate within the fear-paradigm we are frightened, so we become emotionally 'reactive' and our agenda becomes one of just trying to survive the threatening encounter. It is amazing how often we simply fail to consider what outcome we would prefer when we are scared.

On the other hand, within the assertion paradigm we understand there is no threat and so we are able to be 'proactive' and have a more sophisticated strategic plan other than simply 'surviving'. We are able to put our preferred outcome onto the agenda and then fruitfully engage in discussion about its merits or limitations. Mary had a preferred outcome of Tony quitting smoking and she needed to get it onto the agenda.

If we are truly operating assertively then our repertoire

of preferred outcomes would always only ever include win-win solutions. *There is simply no point in considering solutions that do not enhance the other party.* However, it is often necessary to clearly explain the genuine benefits to the other party as the solution may initially appear on the surface to involve unequal effort. This was the case with Mary and Tony, where he may have accidentally thought his preferred outcome was to keep smoking! Tony needed sophisticated, kind and rational persuasion that it was in *his* best interests to put in the extra effort to quit because the outcome would *most* benefit him.

In seeking our preferred outcomes, we also need to ensure they will be good long-term outcomes. We seek solutions that will set us up with new habits that are effective and productive and will enhance us for decades to come. Quitting smoking was Tony's best chance of achieving a productive, healthy and happy life in future decades.

At the same time within the assertion paradigm we are 'realistic' and we accept limitations: no solution is ever perfect, there will always be both negative and positive consequences to any preferred outcome. We simply try to establish through logic, evidence and argument which solution has fewer negative consequences and more positive consequences for both parties. We decide which negative consequences we are willing to live with.

In Tony's case once the arguments were fully consigned the positives were things like better health, improved productivity, more vitality, increased happiness, improved sense of self, improved taking of responsibility, improved relationship with Mary, more closeness, less victim-like passivity and so on.

The negatives for Tony were things like having to struggle to resist urges for nicotine especially during the first few days of withdrawal. Tony would also have to be mentally controlled and not allow himself to pay attention to any mentations in any way related to smoking. In addition, Tony would need to remain alert to the occasional (yet easy to resist) urge that may continue every few months for the next few years. Tony had to be willing to incur these negatives or costs if he was to quit successfully.

These factors make our 'preferred outcome' less straight-forward than we might imagine and certainly not as simple as what we 'want'. Our 'wants' are emotion-based and as a result they are frequently based on old, comfortable, but often useless or self-sabotaging brain habits, like smoking.

TIP THREE: ONLY EVER EXPRESS VULNERABLE EMOTIONS

In ST assertion we often do not need to even mention our emotions. This is particularly the case if we are communicating at work or in other less personal environments. Some of the time, even in personal situations (especially as we get better at assertion) we will not need to discuss our emotions. Basically, as with ST generally, if we change our behaviours we change our brains including our emotions. So often it is just enough to rationally solve a problem and implement behaviour change.

However, when we feel 'stuck' it is often due to our long-harboured emotions. In these cases, we actually need to bring them out of the dark treasure chest where they may have been lurking unchallenged for decades. This is best done with someone who cares about us so that we feel safe – a person who genuinely holds our interests at heart. These treasure chest items need to be subjected to robust critique delivered with kindness.

For example, Mary is soft and kind towards Tony's feelings about why he might have initially started smoking and about how he believes he 'loves' smoking so much that he is 'powerless' to quit. While Mary is kind with Tony, she also gradually helps him to re-evaluate his emotions and to realise he has thus far not subjected his emotions to vigorous critique.

In fact, Mary will argue that it is only his physiological nicotine cravings and urges that are masquerading as intense 'love' feelings and these will largely resolve once the nicotine is out of Tony's system. In other words, Tony is confusing 'loving' smoking with 'withdrawal from nicotine' and subsequent top-up of depleted nicotine levels. Many people associate topping-up their depleted nicotine levels with feelings of 'love' or 'life happiness' but in reality they are just continuing an addictive cycle of an unnecessaty chemical.

Knowing this makes quitting so much easier because

it is only a matter of getting through the withdrawal and our future 'happiness' is not at stake.

Equally, Mary will challenge Tony that it is 100% within his frontal brain control to simply stop paying attention to cigarettes or any mentations related to them and to do this will make quitting actually quite easy. In other words, Mary will emphasise that Tony is not really a powerless victim at all: he has a *genuine* choice and the responsibility for a healthy life lies in his hands.

There may be other occasions also where it is appropriate to express our emotions during conflict. We might do this to 'flag' to the other person that we are on-side with them and we care about them deeply or to indicate the gravity of a situation. What is imperative is that when we do so we express the vulnerable, non-angry, authentic emotion not the deflected, invulnerable emotion particularly as invulnerable emotions support invulnerable behaviours like smoking, drinking alcohol or over-eating.

For example, in the course of their conversations about smoking, Tony might have said things like 'no-one gave a stuff about me when my parents split up', 'it makes me furious to think about it', 'no wonder I took up smoking, it was the only thing that got me through'. Notice that Tony has used words that express the *invulnerable* anger (he is 'furious' no-one 'gave a stuff'). While he keeps telling himself this story (with these invulnerable words) he will continue to blame others and deflect away from his authentic, vulnerable emotion of *sadness* about being left on his own when his parents split.

If Mary were being assertive in this situation she might re-frame Tony's words and analysis at this point by saying something like 'that must have been terribly sad for you, you must have felt so alone – I'm so sorry you had to go through that'. She would pause and let him feel that sadness. Then, most likely Tony would shed a tear or two and he would realise he can actually face his sadness and even start to allow it to heal without having to deflect away from the feeling by using invulnerable words and cigarettes.

In moments of more intense conflict, it is often best not to identify any emotions at all. However, if we feel it is appropriate to do so then it is very important to only ever express the authentic, vulnerable emotion. For example, when the other party expresses an opinion, never say things like 'how dare you' 'that really pisses me off' or 'that makes me furious, annoyed, disappointed, or frustrated'. These are all angry, blaming words that reflect us adopting an aggression strategy and they will escalate the situation so that the other party feels free to use any reciprocating dirty trick they can think of in equally escalating the situation.

Instead express what you *authentically* feel and say things like 'I feel very hurt or upset or all on my own or lonely or really sad'. This allows the other party the opportunity to re-connect with you and see you as a real, living human being who can be hurt and who is not the enemy.

For example, let's say Mary had not conveyed her argument softly enough about how smoking starts to look inadequate as we age. Let's say she said 'You know it really annoys me the way you are looking less and less adequate the older you get by still keeping on smoking'. If Tony were in the fear paradigm he might say 'How dare you, as if you are any more *adequate* than me – what about the way you eat chocolate the whole time, getting fatter and fatter, I suppose that's being 'adequate' is it?'

Notice how by Mary expressing her invulnerable 'annoyance' she has let Tony completely off the hook. He no longer has to engage in debate about the content of her argument. He feels free to escalate for all he is worth. In fact, he may have deliberately goaded and driven Mary to express her 'annoyance' precisely so he gets the relief of being let off the hook.

Not only that, but Tony has also probably successfully de-railed Mary because they are now probably talking about how much chocolate she eats and whether or not she is 'fat'. A golden rule in ST assertion is to *never* get de-railed in an argument.

Where it unintentionally happens then either deal with it immediately 'yes I know 'I' used to smoke too but I also know how unhealthy it made me and that's why I stopped'. On the other hand, if the de-railing will take longer then respond with 'yes, I know that I over-eat chocolate and I know it is not healthy for me, and I am honesty, really happy to talk about that next time we talk, but for the moment let's stay with the smoking issue and she if we can make some progress'.

When Mary temporarily lost mental control and put in the barb about 'annoyance' it allowed Tony to escalate and de-rail. If Mary had not gone briefly into her limbic system and lost control by wanting to punish Tony or if Tony was operating within the assertion paradigm, the outcome would have been different. Tony could have chosen not to escalate and instead expressed vulnerable emotion. He could have said something like 'I feel really hurt and deeply offended that you see me as an inadequate *annoyance* – that really upsets me because I really *love* you'. This response removes the oppositional tone of the interaction, and flags to Mary (if she is responsive) that she got it wrong and was not being kind and soft enough.

Mary could then get back into the assertion paradigm and say something like 'I'm really sorry you are not an annoyance to me at all – I expressed that badly. I love you too, very much'. Then after a pause, she could softly say, 'But we still need to address this issue of others reading you as *inadequate* because it is a reality in our society and it profoundly affects the outcomes you are getting with other people. I want you to do well in life and I don't want you to get blocked by other people. I don't want them to be able to write you off as ineffectual or incompetent. I love you and I am offering to help you with this.'

TIP FOUR: CORRECT ANY ESCALATING BEHAVIOUR *EARLY*

If verbal behaviour escalates we must make sure to correct it early at 3/10 and do not wait till it is higher and less predictable. One way to do this is if the other party escalates in volume then we go quieter but *more pointed and authoritative* in our voice tone in response. Keep in mind that it is hard (but not impossible) to remain escalated if you are the only one who is losing control.

In these situations, we can also make eye contact, show the hand palms to the escalating party (as a containing gesture) and say with all seriousness in an authoritative voice things like 'That's not okay, you need to keep control of your own emotions ... I'm happy to talk about this but we need to stay kind and friendly'. If the escalation continues then close the argument and put in place a clear negative consequence, like leaving the situation.

TIP FIVE: ASSERTION WITHIN HIERARCHIES

Hierarchies are a reality of life and we often have to operate within them. Even though in hierarchies equity and fairness may not always prevail, in ST assertion we still adopt an egalitarian style at a personal level in our communication style. We debate the issues as equals assuming equal levels of rationality and logic and fair rules of engagement. However, even though the most persuasive argument may not always be adopted by people above us in the hierarchy we still have a responsibility to identify any negative consequences we can foresee with their choices.

For example, we may say 'I'm very happy to work on this project you have identified as a priority, but it will mean that my progress on these other jobs will be slower. Even with very hard work on my part, this other project (which I believe is important to you) will not be able to be completed for many months given this new one. Are you okay with that?'

In a different situation we might say 'Yes, I can see why you would like to put that information into the press release but I am concerned that it might be misinterpreted by the public and reflect poorly on our department. I think with a bit more work we could maybe find a way to say this differently so we can avoid any undesired outcomes'.

TIP SIX: UNDERSTATE OUR CASE AND USE INDISPUTABLE, VERBATIM EVIDENCE

When we are defensive it is easy to use words that over-state our case and make our argument difficult to defend. It is often best to eliminate these types of extreme words from our repertoire in many circumstances. For example, it is can be lethal to use words like 'always' or 'never' as it is very easy to find exceptions. In arguments we often hear people say things like 'You always defend him, you never defend me' which is just like giving an open invitation to the other party to (unnecessarily) destroy your case or derail the argument onto whether or not there are exceptions. Instead we might use words like 'quite often' or 'some of the time' even where the event is highly frequent. In most cases, an under-stated case is far more persuasive.

Where possible, use indisputable, verbatim evidence

to describe a problem. People frequently go back to evidence that occurred decades ago and over which there will be no agreement or witnesses, such as 'even when I was a child you were always horrible to me, always being critical and mean'. In preference, it would be better not to delve back into the murky past but rather to note the ongoing problem. For example, 'we have been sitting here for about half an hour and in that time you first said I was insensitive, then you secondly said my husband had a lot to put up with, then you thirdly said I looked bad in these clothes and you have just finished saying I'm lazy. These are all examples of your hostility towards me. We might note that in that same time period I have not make a single critical comment about you. On this evidence I find it extraordinary that you say I am the one who is *always* mean to you'.

TIP SEVEN:
NO HIDDEN 'BARBS'

People are not stupid. Hidden barbs do not go unnoticed and they will escalate the situation in subtle ways such as increasing passive resistance or blocking and they will make cooperation untenable. When we use them we tend to end up with lose-lose outcomes. They are a failure of proper mental control and we must resist these limbic system urges to have that nasty little snide dig at the other party even when we feel upset and hurt.

Moreover, hidden barbs are against our own best interests. Using them allows us to avoid taking proper responsibility. We cannot easily solve problems when we fail to own up to our own agenda. ST assertion is about transparent, open, direct communication it is not about passive aggression and half saying something mean and then claiming we 'didn't mean it'. That's for babies.

TIP EIGHT: THE IMPORTANCE OF BOTH GOODWILL AND WALKING AWAY

The extent to which we are willing to keep discussing and ironing out issues will depend upon the overall quality of the relationship and the amount of accumulated goodwill as well as the benefits we stand to gain from resolution. This means that in some cases we might prefer to spend thirty years making a significant contribution to the wider world through our career rather than spend that time endlessly trying to resolve dysfunctional relationships. We have limited time and choices to make.

Some ineffectual relationships might be let go or maintained only at a fairly superficial level. This is fine. Obviously though, where there is a strong *mutual* interest in a high quality, fair and equal relationship then the effort on both sides to resolve issues will be stronger.

Often people try to pretend that relationships are

more than what they actually are, so we must get real. If relationships are not mutually satisfying then we can stop flogging a dead horse and walk away. This is part of being proactive and knowing we have choices. When relationships are not satisfying that is a clear and foreseeable consequence of both people's behaviour. Relationships can only be what each party is prepared to put in.

When we observe that the other party fails to put in enough, we ought to allow the relationship to reflect that and lose some interest ourselves. In relationships we initiate interactions roughly equally, so we should not keep making overture after overture without proper reciprocity. If the disinterest continues then we accept reality and lose all interest ourselves and walk away. In ST assertion, while we are keen to cooperate we can equally walk away especially if we are being treated poorly. Our self-respect ultimately takes priority over any need for a relationship.

TIP NINE: THE IMPORTANCE OF OPENLY ASKING FOR FAVOURS

Most relationships are based on fairness and equal contribution. Often when people operate within the fear paradigm they see others as the opposition and therefore do not want to acknowledge any 'debt' by asking for favours openly. However, not to ask openly makes other people feel that their help is going unacknowledged. In ST assertion asking openly for favours ensures that other people feel their help is being transparently noted as *their* contribution. When favours are not openly asked for other people feel resentful, and this reduces goodwill and lowers our motivation to cooperate.

For example, if we would like to have our grass cut around our home we do *not* say 'Do you want to come over and help me mow the lawn?' This slight of hand is damaging for two obvious reasons. Firstly, because it suggests the other person *wants* to come over and mow our lawn when it is really that we want our grass cut. Secondly, by saying 'help me' we are *minimising the task* by suggesting that we will also be mowing the lawn and the other person is just helping.

Instead it would be better to say 'I am just wondering if there is any possibility that you could come over to mow my lawn. I would really appreciate it because my knee is giving me lots of trouble at the moment. No problems at all if you can't as I know you are very busy at the moment'. This is transparent, non-demanding and it gives the other person an easy way of saying no. Within ST assertion, all parties need to know they have choices and are not pressured or compelled towards a single outcome.

TIP TEN: THE IMPORTANCE OF PROPER APOLOGY

So many people struggle to apologise, yet it is a crucial aspect of the ST assertion paradigm. We all behave badly at times but that is not the problem. It is the failure to accept responsibility and acknowledge our mistake that is the problem. Also, often people deliver 'pretend' apologies like 'I'm sorry but you made me do it' or 'I'm sorry but you're just too sensitive'. These are examples of yet another attack being disguised or 'dressed up' as an apology and to use them will severely damage goodwill and cooperation and generally result in lose-lose outcomes.

On the other hand, apologies can include qualifications or explanations in complex situations. Sometimes explanations provide more richness and increase understanding of the problematic behaviour which is often helpful. For example, 'I'm sorry I got annoyed it wasn't fair. I think I may have been overtired which made me overreact.

I'll make sure it doesn't happen again.' This explanation is helpful because it allows the person who is apologising to understand (for future benefit) that getting annoyed is often preceded by getting overtired which will help them to ensure fewer repetitions. It is important though that any qualifications or explanations do not negate the apology.

It is in everyone's best interests to apologise for several reasons. Firstly, it is not until we acknowledge our problematic behaviours and take responsibility for them that we are able to learn from them and move forwards. So an apology cannot be a general apology like 'I'm sorry for everything' (this is another 'pretend' apology) it needs to identify the specific problematic behaviour.

Secondly, an apology very importantly, allows us to forgive ourselves which means we can reduce the amount of guilt and self-blame we hold giving us the freedom to move forward emotionally.

Thirdly, it allows other people to genuinely forgive us and not harbour hidden resentment which might otherwise be played out in interactions going forward. This is because a proper apology takes responsibility, identifies the problem behaviour, acknowledges the harm done to the other person and endeavours to correct future behaviour.

A proper apology looks something like 'I'm sorry I behaved badly when I drove too fast with you in the car. It wasn't fair of me and I know it frightened you. I won't ever allow that to happen again. Please forgive me.'

TIP ELEVEN: CONTROL WHAT WE CAN, LET GO OF WHAT WE CANNOT

Finally, be aware that in most cases we can strongly influence outcomes. In other cases we cannot influence outcomes, or we could, but we are not willing to do what is required to influence the outcome. This is our choice, we are mostly not victims, so there is little point complaining about things we are unwilling to change.

In life, it is wise to accept and let go of what we cannot change or are not willing to change and instead focus and work hard on what we can change.

Printed in Australia
AUOW01n0006240918
303087AU00003B/6